WRITERS WITHOUT MARGINS®
A Journal of Poetry and Prose

VOLUME IV
The Human/Nature Edition

Editor
Cheryl Buchanan

Assistant Editors
Olivia Loftis
Kelsey Day Marlett
Olivia Smith

for

**Christine
Christopher
and
Daniel**

We Would Like to Extend Our Appreciation To:

The Harmon Foundation, once again, for their financial support to make the printing of this collection possible

Our Workshop Facilitators: Kaylee Anzick, Bassam Attia, Faith Breisblatt, Olivia Kate Cerrone, Susan Cheever, Evan Jymaal Cutts, Andrew Dunn, Lauren Lopez, Mark MacNeil, Caitlin McGill, Kevin McLellan, Skoot Mosby, Zachary Paul, Kenny Pina, Amanda Role, Max Smith, Massiel Torres Ulloa, and Mathematics Millionaire X

Our Program Partners: Donna Miller, Ben Wade, Tatiana Taforo, Shivon Olivier, Rosa Pichardo, Al Flint, Daniela Carrasquillo, Ligia Tjada and Chris Carrasquillo at the Wyman Recovery Home; Kat James, Alice Tilton and Nate Pally at Bridge Over Troubled Waters; Diane Delehanty and Karen Seck at The Center for Change; Linda Dolph and Fabiana Videla at St. Francis House; Rachel Gannon at Pine Street; and Emily Gordon at the Boston Public Library

Our Board Members: Stephen Kennedy Smith, Theo Theoharis, Lucinda Jewel and Natalia Livingston

Our Contributors: To learn more about this year's selected authors, please see the "Our Contributors" section in the back of this journal

And, Special Thanks to: Thomas McNeely, as our current liaison with Emerson College, Tom Johnston in the Mayor's Office of Arts and Culture, Suchita Chadha for lending her talents in graphic design, and Stephen Crivellaro for spearheading our marketing and communications

Cover art and illustrations by Lillian Young-Fritchie

© 2019 by Writers Without Margins, Inc.

Nature teaches more than she preaches.
-John Burroughs

Editor's Note:

This year's journal, with 37 contributors and 13 returning writers submitting from 6 of our workshops in Greater Boston, presents as our biggest and boldest edition yet. And, although the following pages may demonstrate a year of stability and growth in our programs, they are also a window into the complicated, and often dangerous, world we inhabit. This year, two of our contributors were incarcerated. One returned. One very likely may not. This year, three of our workshop participants fatally overdosed. Two have submissions in the journal. One did not have time. In communities where incarceration is far too expected, in a year where overdose statistics are higher than ever, we can't expect alarming facts to be merely distant figures. These are not just numbers, but friends we are sitting next to in our workshops, and they have reached out to offer their writing to you.

Each year, we look at the overall theme of the collection after reviewing submissions, rather than asking for contributors to submit works related to a particular idea. I would not have predicted that the predominant theme of this year's journal would have been interconnectedness with one another and the natural world. But, undeniably, it is. Furthermore, this emerged not from similar prompts or responses inspired by the same poems, but across different groups through unrelated conversations. Over and over, the power and majesty of an ever-present, indefatigable, and sometimes mystical relationship with the natural world is reimagined and recreated, here, through the writing process. There is also evidence of a sort of will that transcends physical frailty and vulnerability. Some might call this *hope*. There seems to be a broader, universal possibility posed for humanity as members of something larger here, even if complete understanding may be just out of reach. Nonetheless, we keep reaching.

Cheryl Buchanan, JD, MFA
Executive Director and Workshop Facilitator

CONTENTS

Ayanna Holder
Window of Truth — 15

I. AIR

M.R. Shipp
Reading on a Wintery Day — 19

Michael K. Capriola, Jr.
To Understand Houses — 21

Stephen Crivellaro
Unsolicited Solitude Shattered
by Kind Words and a Gentle Heart — 22

Adam Ferreira
Steps for Telling a Joke — 24

Martin Rodriguez
Conference Call — 25

Lisa Harding
Connection! — 27

Michael K. Capriola, Jr.
Untitled — 28

Cheryl Blanchard
Declaration of Cheryl — 29

Mark Taylor
The Greatest Story Untold — 30

Cles Wilson
If Only   31

I Confess My Sadness to the Sound
William Sharp   33

II. EARTH

Brian Bellamy
Bricks Set in Dirt   37

Beatrice Greene
Remember   38

Andrew Burlile
What Writing Is   39

William
The Room   43

Laura Price
Family Repairs   44

Beatrice Greene
No Windows, No Doors   45

Sara Willig
Doing Weird Jobs for
Strange People for Little Pay   46

Karen Brogan
Just Me   47

Zachary Alonzo
from Imagine This: The First Twenty-Four   48

Kay Bluelondon
The American Wheel   51

T. O'Malley
Recovery Smart Book on Being Found   52

Kevin Reddick
To Be Honest   53

L. Marcel Harrison
Blessings   54

III. FIRE

Zachary Alonzo
How to Be the Change   57

L. Marcel Harrison
1-5   58

Adam Ferreira
Nobody Ever Likes a Mockingbird   60

Mathematics Millionaire X
Addiction   61

L. Marcel Harrison
Don't Just Survive   63

Joel Thompson
The Prophet of Poison, II   64

Brian Bellamy
Disgusting   66

Malik Hall
Confessions of a Couch Potato　　　67

Mark Taylor
Saw It in a Dream　　　68

Barbara Lewis
The Still　　　70

Christine Arrington
Untitled　　　74

IV. WATER

Tyson
An Open Letter to Me, Myself, and I　　　77

Ayanna Holder
Hope Fade, Time Slayed　　　79

Bassam Attia
The Visit　　　80

Evan Jymaal Cutts
Chance Encounter　　　81

Anthony Calhoun
Evans is a Poet: A Literary Analysis
of "Chance Encounter"　　　83

Debbie Wiess
Whistler's Nocturne　　　84

Daniel
Untitled I   87

Wyman Group 2
Yet Another Exquisite Corpse   88

City World
In the Ocean   89

Bruce DiGaetano, II
As Deep as Earth Below the Ocean   90

Adam Ferreira
Spawn Season   91

Sara Willig
HaT'Keyah: Grumpy Jew Poem #89   92

Joel Reyes, Jr.
Poetic Medicine   93

V. OUR CONTRIBUTORS   95

VI. OUR PARTNERS   107

VII. OUR MISSION   111

WINDOW OF TRUTH

Ayanna Holder

A star, a beam of light, a being of what's good
in the world soaring through time though young
she is old to this sphere of fire   earth   water   and air.
One sees a violent person, but she sees a Soul tainted
when still pure at heart. For life is a game,
our years the many levels   the trials
the adventures   the choices
the game board of several paths.

I. AIR

READING ON A WINTERY DAY

M.R. Shipp

In its migratory winds and
solitary white sheets,
this winter day
gave her an easy lover
named reading
and drove her resentful,
beautiful cat to the television set
in the other room.
Outspread brightness
from the morning sunlight
pierced the darkness in her retreat
and roused her.
A day abandoned to reading.
And, while Sammy the cat skirted,
Roger the dog stood,
inert and happy,
next to her bed anxious for his clue,
spooking
her with those big hearted eyes
and guiding her to the chilly window
with a warm bark
where breathing winds
blow snowflakes off
to a familiar and unfamiliar immortality.
Elizabeth sprung to the day
with two books on her brain
one fresh, one unfinished,
Romance and the Cosmos.
Face and body washed,
and now with full coffee mug,
she is back in her bed,

the electronic tablet is already there
and she signals her two books into existence.
The dog is at her side with his e-book too,
phantom reading eyes cuddled onto the screen.
Elizabeth and Roger in their cold season cave,
cut off from ordinary time for winter and words,
self-reliant and oblivious to all things except
the pure delight of reading!

TO UNDERSTAND HOUSES

Michael K. Capriola, Jr.

You must venture into the kitchen,
the place where people might come
for food and drink,
for warmth of hearth,
for warmth of companionship.

Nowadays the women gather at the kitchen table
while the men cluster before the TV in the den
where the game holds them in thrall
(harking back to his and hers campfires on the
Savannah).

The children are floating
between these two worlds,
their steps taking them
from kitchens to dens, and the rooms between
and into the yard's outside houses
and back inside again,
flitting in and out
of curious holes in the world.

UNSOLICITED SOLITUDE SHATTERED BY KIND WORDS AND A GENTLE HEART

Stephen Crivellaro

Sometimes,
the Miracle really does happen,
when you least expect it,
by who you least expected.
You see,
it doesn't take much to transform someone's life,
so much so,
that sometimes it happens
without actually even trying to.

My Miracle
came in the form of an Angel
sent down to rescue me
when my hope had all but vanished.
Just Imagine,
if I had I never walked into the room that day,
or
had I never summoned up the Courage that night.
Where would I be?
Who would I be?

Those questions provoke another thought,
because
who I was yesterday,
Is not who I am today.

And, who I am today,
will not be who I am tomorrow,

What we choose,

no matter how insignificant we feel it is,
affects the lives of those around us.
Every gentle touch, every kind word,
every selfless act,
affects the trajectory of life itself.
So remember,
people matter, Angels matter,
the choices we make matter.
Choose to do the right thing,
even when no one is watching.

The momentum my life has today,
inspires me in ways I didn't know were possible.
I just hope that one day,
I'll be in the position to give back,
and to share with others,
just a fraction,
of what was so graciously shared to me.

STEPS FOR TELLING A JOKE

Adam Ferreira

Step #1: crack a joke at someone
Step #2: hope it don't offend
Step #3: who cares if it does
Step #4: crack another joke
Step #5: hope it offends
Step #6: laugh about it
Step #7: keep cracking jokes
Step #8: get recipient of said jokes to finally laugh
Step #9: if that don't work, give up or...
Step #10: take it too far
Step #11: try not to offend too much
Step #12: get real vicious with jokes
Step #13: when situation gets outta hand, throw in the bombshell
Step #14: regret the hurt you've caused in people's lives
Step #15: repair

CONFERENCE CALL

Martin Rodriguez

Mother: "I think this nursing home is closing. The food isn't too good anymore."
Daughter: "Try having Stage 4 cancer with chemo. I can hardly eat a thing."
Son: "Ma, that place has a waiting list. It's harder to get into than Harvard."

Mother: "They don't give you much: a few strips of chicken, some mashed potatoes."
Daughter: "I feel nauseous all the time. I've lost fifty pounds."
Son: "Ma, they'll give you more if you ask. Whatever you want, they'll make it."

Mother: "I almost choked on the ten pills I took this morning."
Daughter: "They say you're hardly on any compared to the other patients."
Son: "Ma, some of those pills are just vitamins."

Mother: "My roommate's dressers take up the whole room."
Daughter: "Your health insurance paperwork is all over my kitchen table."
Son: "Ma, I had them give you a new table with some shelves."

Mother: "That's alright. I don't care about decorating anymore."
Daughter: "I don't care either. Do you think I care?"

Son: "*Ma, I put your dolls and your photo album on the shelves.*"
Mother: "Well, you just eat well, that's all."
Daughter: "I always did, and a lot of good it did me."
Son: "*Ma, have they been bringing you to physical therapy?*"

Mother: "You always ate crap, ever since you were little."
Daughter: "Oh, I know, so it's my fault I got cancer."
Son: "*Ma, we shouldn't bother Laura about her diet.*"

Mother: "I found a piece of chocolate on the floor, and I ate it."
Daughter: "You always had candy, cakes - when did you ever go without?"
Son: "*Ma, I could bring you a sleeve of Pym's chocolate cookies.*"

Mother: "My brother's so smart, getting us all on the phone at once."
Daughter: "He's always been your favorite."
Son: "*Ma, I'm not your brother, I'm your only son.*"

CONNECTION!

Lisa Harding

I am the animal of your imagination
Think of your body as an animal, a soft and strong animal
Use your imagination to make yourself better
Let your loneliness be your landscape
You don't have to be perfect
Announce your despair to the rain
The world goes wild. The world goes on.

UNTITLED

Michael K. Capriola, Jr.

1)
The birds chatter their excitement
while trees quietly produce buds.
snow melts, rain comes;
There is mud everywhere.
Note to self:
Buy a mop,
put the winter coat away.

2)
Fantastic ferns frequently never fade.

3)
Practice eulogies.
We need some for the prominent leader
and renowned statesman who recently passed away.
Heads of state & diplomats & such
will come to the funeral
to pay their last respects.
and to make sure he's dead.

4)
Leaves in wind reveal themselves
as spirited, dancing in circles across the pavement
the gust of wind providing the music,
the catalyst,
inspiring the leaves in their joyful play.

DECLARATION OF CHERYL

Cheryl Blanchard

I enjoy Candy Crusher
And I am a Woman

I wear Watches of all Colors and Kinds
I am a Woman

I am a loyal Friend, whenever you need me
And I am a Woman!

I have stood in the face of Adversity
And I am a Woman!

I have suffered the loss of my Children,
the loss of my Parents
And I am a Woman!

I collect Angels, Angels everywhere
And I am a Woman

I am a Woman
I will Not be Stopped!

THE GREATEST STORY UNTOLD

Mark Taylor

In a similar fashion as Muhammad Ali, who proclaimed triumphantly in the boxing arena,
"I am the Greatest," another notable man, Barack Obama, first Black American in history is elected to the highest office of U.S. President.

Times' lapsed. My story has evolved. My immensity among the scribes I humbly proclaim. Yet, I implore you, don't count me out. I've erred. So have we all. Learning from mistakes is what life's about. Keenly aware, on occasion I'll be tense. It is then that my weakness becomes my strength. Behold, the character produced, valuable nuggets of wisdom implemented to facilitate the unfolding of the greatest story, which must not go untold.

IF ONLY,

Cles Wilson

We had stopped, and listened

Listened and Learned

Learned and Empowered.

BUT

We didn't … Did We?

INSTEAD

At the very bottom of a voided pit

Starkness seeps to where…

Restless pain rises up to an 8 octave range

AND THEY CONTINUE

To do damage

On things we cannot speak of

To the law we bow down

As the afflicted move forward

Into more re-addictive afflictions

WHILE WE

Who had to come into existence

Watch and Wait,

Wait and Watch,

And earn pats-on-the-back hurrahs

As the cycle of choice

OR

Is it the choice of the cycle?

Runs in many different directions

I CONFESS MY SADNESS TO THE SOUND

William Sharp

Sad is something I unfortunately keep around. One wrong step, I try to keep as a reminder for that step will lead to confinement. Is it the step that keeps me unhappy or is it myself that forces me to feel crappy? Emptiness is a sound that can be heard for miles. Is it from the echo, or lack of smiles? If writing had one reason to rhyme, it would be for me wasting way too much time. Fortunately, I've given myself another chance. It's up to only me to take that stance. I long to lose the sadness so deep that it's in my soul. I need to really hurry, for I'm only getting old.

II. EARTH

BRICKS SET IN DIRT

Brian Bellamy

Brick set in dirt
with weeds and moss
growing in between

in the cracks

I don't remember
what was said or done
having to remove everything

in the cracks

Or how long
how many times repeated
that action took place digging

in the cracks

It got done grudgingly
and when that happened I could go play
after it was clean

in the cracks

REMEMBER

Beatrice Greene

Remember the women who dared

to speak, to be.

Their stories and ours

must be told again and again

to break the grip of silence

from without and within.

We place our ears to the ground

listen to rhythms of Nature

and Earth, both our mothers.

Gathering strength from just

below our navels

we stand shoulder to shoulder then kneel

to doula each other into new life

we women of all colors, beliefs,

we women of all nations.

WHAT WRITING IS

Andrew Burlile

Do you experience intense feelings of doom? Overwhelming emotions? Racing thoughts? If so then you may be eligible to participate in a two-week study on anti-anxiety medication overseen by

The words are slight. Sans-serif. Nonthreatening, a dark grey font nearly indistinguishable from black, printed on an off-white banner, placed carefully just above commuters' heads on the T. I glance back from the ad to the other passengers. They pack closely together, standing, or sitting, either staring out the window or oscillating between their phone or book to the outside and back. A few sway with the car's gravity. I sway with them.

The T stops. We cluster to let more on. I feel bad for the woman who stood under my arm; I had showered, but I hadn't washed my shirt in a week. The car jolts on. We all watch the trees roll up behind concrete as we descend into Kenmore. Underground the B-line sheds brownstone for a bright blackness. All you have to look at is your phone, or the darkness outside the window which reflects your own image. Or the ads.

I hadn't seen this one before. I first noticed it when I got on in Allston, where, next to me, with me, pushing into the trolley, others held up their wallets and flashed their Charlie Cards and I did the same knowing full well I didn't have the fare if the driver were to ask me to come to the front.

The ad continued. *For participation you may be eligible for a cash compensation up to $300.*
Up to. What made someone eligible for the full amount? To what would you need to agree?

When I worked as a linguistic researcher at Virginia Tech, I took an IRB certification course which forbade unethical practices, such as offering financial compensation that was "undeniable." I make $11 hour. My net pay comes to perhaps $400 biweekly. Not including tips.

The same year I earned IRB certification, a friend of mine at another university, studying in one of the country's top biomedical programs, called to ask my opinion about sperm donation. When I pressed him for a reason he responded that it's "more enjoyable than donating plasma."

The B-line ends at Park Street. It doesn't venture into the financial district. You won't see anyone wearing suits on the B-line unless they got on at Hynes (having taken from Harvard the #1 bus – one: superlative, generative, capital). The Green Line intersects at Park Street with the Red Line, which veins all the way from Alewife to Braintree. For $2.25 you could observe the creep of gentrification from north to south, east to west.

Was this ad for me? Because it felt "undeniable." $300 was grocery money for three months. Or it was a fifth of one month's rent.

I did not come to Boston impoverished. I came with savings. I came, I thought, ready for its challenges. But coming to Boston is like riding the B-line. You get on in Allston, riding through the gentrified grit of performative punk and you feel empowered by a diversity which feels comfortable to a white southern boy like you, because it's diversity in moderation. The Orthodox Jewish neighborhood and the Orthodox Russian butcher, the Korean barbecues and three Starbucks are all a type of familiarity which affords a comfortable participation in gentrification under another umbrella term: "just getting by." I joke at work that I'm not wealthy enough to have ethics. I can't buy reusable bags. I moonlight in my head that I write a polemic about the microplastics found in oysters. Op-eds for the *Globe*. Which lead to a book deal at Knopf. A PEN/Faulkner. Eventually a National Book Award. At the same time I imagine writing this piece, I also imagine eating the oyster. Relishing the brine. I like to know my oysters were bottom-feeders.

But then the B-line slips out of Allston and into Boston, passed the theatres of BU, by the sanctuary of the MFA you were not accepted into. The ramen place you've wanted to try but can't afford. And then you descend into that lambent darkness.

When the windows go dark, I won't lie, I look at the reflections of others. I see others glance above my head. They linger. I linger on them. How they turn their whole bodies away from the banner. I know they're also from Allston by how they linger, as if they're waiting for the change of stoplight to cross.

After ending the call with my friend, who ultimately backed out of donating sperm, I looked up clinics nearby. One of them offered up to $1000 a month for regular donations.

Up to. A phrase that indicates potential, but with no promise of achieving it. It's the American Dream in a word. It's also an idiom; what are you up to? (Oh, just getting by.) Lastly it's an implication of collusion. Up to something. The suspicion of artifice, of subterfuge, of clever misdirection. The very same sleight-of-hand I used to design the linguistic research project. IRB protocol permitted outright equivocation to the participant so long as they were not harmed. And so long as the compensation was never undeniable.

What is the threshold at which an offer becomes undeniable? At what price are we willing to sell our neurochemistry? What risks are we willing to incur? By advertising on the T – to those who can afford Allston, but suffer it – the ad suggests those who can be bought are coming from Allston, from Roxbury, from Forest Hills. And that researchers know how to coerce them.

Is that what research is? The practice of displacing your own curiosity on the bodies of others. A type of voyeurism that is hypothetically consensual. Another brand of gentrification. Pretending to look out the window to look back at those around you.

I write down the number. At the bottom of the ad, in a crimson banner, Harvard Medical printed their seal: VE RI TAS.

THE ROOM

William

The room can never be
forgotten it was in this
room that my demands
surfaced. Where I so clearly
saw the shattered fabric of
my soul. Where I
felt the pain in its
fullness and most penetrating.
Where silent
Screams of agony went unheard.

FAMILY REPAIRS

Laura Price

On February 20, I was sitting in my wooden chair in my room and had just finished eating my blueberry yogurt and pepperoni hot pocket. My cell phone rang. I answered the phone and said hello. It was my sister. I was very happy to hear from her. It had been a long 12 years. We talked about my current situation and then she asked me about why I left Lynn six years ago. Then she asked me about Kevin.

"Was he doing drugs when I came by your house in Lynn?"

"Yes."

She took a deep breath in. I was still sitting in my chair.

Then she asked me, "Do you wear TEDs stockings?"

"Yes," I told her.

"I wear them for my veins," she said. She made me laugh because of what she said next. "When I take the stockings off, I sit on the bed and start to fart. I almost surprise myself. I laugh so hard that I have to cross my legs."

I was in stitches.

Then she said, "The doctor tells me that I have to wear them two times a day and I do not like THAT." The conversation shifted again and she said, "I have a black cat named Lunar and she sits on the recliner chair and meows to tell me that the box needs to be changed. But when Lunar meows loud, she wants to eat. Lunar and I have talking matches. It's ok, as long as the cat doesn't talk back."

I asked if I could see her. And she said, "In the future. Let's see how things go."

NO WINDOWS, NO DOORS

Beatrice Greene

Viewing the McLeod Plantation, James Island, South Carolina, online

Where people ate, slept, had sex, babies and died,
four walls, a roof, an entryway
no windows, no doors.

I felt closed in, one eye weeps the other dry;
a strong urge to vomit sadness and anger away
but I must honor the feelings the endurance of

real people toiling to make others rich.
I want to stab at ghosts of slave masters
who could be in my DNA.

As property the captor's the owner's
came and for pleasure and by right
no windows, no doors.

DOING WEIRD JOBS FOR STRANGE PEOPLE FOR LITTLE PAY

Sara Willig

My first service job was in the mid-80s, during a month-long internship between semesters with a group, Community for Creative Non-Violence, which fed the homeless in downtown D.C.—forcing the suits to see what was preferred to be kept invisible. Upon my arrival, the man who picked me up at the airport asked me, "Are you Jewish, or vegetarian? Almost everyone who comes here is one or the other...or both."

My second service job was in an institution in 1990 - The Ivy Street School. Everyone was Gay, Lesbian, Immigrant, and/or Minority. I applied for this job from the paper, thinking it was the only thing I was qualified for after dropping out of two undergrad programs in quick succession. Having a disabled sibling was my qualification. The job didn't require nice clothes. How could it when human bodily fluids were always to be dealt with? This was before OSHA and we had no gloves or bio-waste bags. I got worms twice, no, three times.

These were jobs I couldn't geek about with my non-work friends. Can't talk about getting bit. Can't talk about having to do three-person restraints. Can't talk about what having no corpus callosum does to a person. Can't talk about shit-smearing. Can't talk about having learned to diaper on a hairy adult. Can't talk about hours spent keeping a person from hitting his own ears. Who could relate?

JUST ME

Karen Brogan

You do not have to walk on your knees,
unless God didn't give you feet when you were born.

My brother was born with square knees
he couldn't keep up with others
but with braces, he tried.

If you go out into the world,
you have to know what you're doing:
have a schedule, a purpose, an agenda.

I learned to live with the reality of losing my parents
and to live on.

When my parents were not there to coach me,

I had to turn to strangers.

The world is big
You have to learn to get along.

Sometimes when I think of my parents
I feel lonely.

from IMAGINE THIS: THE FIRST TWENTY-FOUR

Zachary Alonzo

About 9:30 p.m., August 27, 2014

I step down from the back of a cramped van, shackles clanging, taking small steps. I'm told to walk 25 **feet** or so, through a door, and down 20 **to** 30 steps. I try to balance myself with my hands stuck to my side, and I'm placed in a small room. The door is shut behind me. I need to go to the bathroom, but there's nowhere to go.

Not sure how much later, I'm pulled out of the room, brought to a metal bench, cuffs and shackles are finally removed, arms and legs are finally able to move freely, as freely as they're going to be able to for the next two years or so. I'm then brought behind a **three-foot** wall and told to strip down naked.

"Open mouth."
"Lift arms."
"Lift," (points at my crotch).
"Turn around."
"Lift feet."
"Squat and cough."

I'm given a cheap pair of used green top and bottoms, a white t-shirt, some boxers, socks, and shoes that might as well be winter-weight socks. I don't have to use the bathroom anymore; I'm too terrified. They put me back in the room.

I'm pulled back out of the room again and brought to speak with a "nurse" about any health issues. I'm given a TB test and sent on to the next person who explains the "rules and regulations" and all this other nonsense that sounds crazy, and quickly I'm brought over to have my picture taken. I'm told to stand still, see a mouse go running across the floor, and FLASH! It's obvious from the expression on my face in the picture, but the officer won't change it for me. I'm given an ID with this picture, my basic information, and the number w105067, which is pretty much how I'll be referenced for a while, and they put me back in the room.

Back out of the room again, and I'm given a laundry bag full of more used tops and bottoms, white t-shirts, boxers, socks, "toiletries," a pad of yellow paper, envelopes, and a pen that's impossible to write with. There's also a brown paper bag with warm milk, two stale cookies, an apple that might be two years old, and one slice of bologna on stale wheat bread. Next is a piece of paper with a copy of my ID, "B-2" written on it.

Maybe 11:00 p.m., August 27, 2014

I'm brought to a barred, metal door with the label B-2 above it. The door is opened. I walk in. Most of the lights are out, there's lots of yelling, but I can see three levels on the right and metal tables, with chairs attached, straight ahead. I hand my paper to a man and am told to go to #6. I walk over to #6 and, after about five minutes, the door slowly slides open. I step in. It closes behind me.

There's a bunk bed on my left, a metal toilet straight ahead, a metal desk with a broken chair on my right, and a small shelf with four hooks up high above it. I dump out the laundry bag and realize there's also a set of sheets that feel like paper and I put them on a slab of a mattress on the bottom bunk, which is labeled 6a. I make the bed to the best of my ability and a pillow out of the extra clothes I was given. I can't eat, so I lie down and try to sleep. I stare at the ceiling and listen to the yelling.

7:00 a.m., August 28, 2014 (found out exact time later)

All the doors start opening but #6 stays closed. A couple of guys in the unit ask the person in charge to open my door for me. 10 minutes later, it's finally realized that the person in charge last night didn't mark that #6 was now occupied and the door opens. About **10 to 15 other** guys ask me where I'm from, not caring what my name is, and one guy tells me it's about to be chow time. I watch on as everyone else basically stands behind a yellow line, waiting to be called. "Chow!" is yelled, and the door of B-2 is opened.

Everyone files out to the hallway, through the metal detector, and down to the chow hall. Breakfast is dry cereal, a piece of cake, and two barely cold cartons of milk. I sit by myself. I don't know a single person.

I barely eat, hand my tray to a man at the back of the chow hall, and walk back to B-2. I see other men checking a paper with names and numbers on it, so I find my name on the list and a number, with *Orientation 10:00 a.m.* written next to it. Another ten or so guys ask me where I'm from and I hear, "10 o'clock movement," announced. I leave B-2 and go to the auditorium for orientation. They tell us to sit every other seat and we watch two videos. One about the facility. One about prison rape.

THE AMERICAN WHEEL

Kay Bluelondon

The sky is a never-ending
masterpiece while the land
seeks to be hidden from being
exploited for its rich soil.

Men, looking to find a place to worship God
in their own way and a place to call Home,
got greed, forgot the American Wheel
that put them on their feet and made
this country great. Bring back the American Wheel.

On display at the Fuller Craft Museum, Recent Acquisitions Exhibit, 2018

RECOVERY SMART BOOK ON BEING FOUND
T. O'Malley

1. Go blindly into recovery
2. Freak out, wake a buddy, bring a battalion of like-minded addicts
3. Certainly, it isn't your first time in a program
4. When you're asked to speak in front of a group for the first time, you know you're screwed
5. You sit in the back, but you want to be noticed
6. Withdrawals at night feel like stabbing knives
7. That's a lot of pain
8. Spread disinformation about your drug use. Don't make it easy on yourself
9. Or others, for that matter
10. Technically, you're an adult, but you still act like a child
11. You can leave at any time, but when you return, you'll go to prison
12. Did your parents envision this life for you?
13. *Straight* means high / *straight* also means sober
14. Thank you, English class
15. When you shoot, you shoot yourself
16. With no signposts, you start your journey aimlessly
17. Abstinence doesn't mean sobriety
18. You will plunge into despair, feel utterly alone
19. The light in the distance is Peace
20. You're made to think alike, but in the end, you find your true inner self

TO BE HONEST

Kevin Reddick

I have a lot to say
but God's words are more
honest and true.
Who will believe
in what I have to say,
because God's words are more
honest and true?
If I listen
to what He has to say
then maybe my words
will be too.

BLESSINGS

L. Marcel Harrison

Blessings bestowed yesterday
are just as relevant today.

They should be relived
in spirit as often as
memory will allow

but never forget.

III. FIRE

HOW TO BE THE CHANGE

Zachary Alonzo

No Fear at All
Back from the Dead
Not too Fast
Put up the Barricades

Breaking Free from the Cell
Multiple Complications
A Brief History of the Crisis is Needed
Knowing not Guessing

Safer than it was;
But Crises have a Habit of Recurring
Slave to the Algorithm

Fuel of the Future
Doing Good, Doing Well
Processing the Progress
Big is Beautiful

Any Questions?!

1-5

L. Marcel Harrison

1. nothing
Title, first full of perception.
Nothing means exactly that, period.

2.1 neutrality
Neither here nor there, with true contentment
or fear, self-doubt, lack of enlightenment.

2.2 minimization
Taking the least amount
with the greater value
and maximizing its use and appearance
for total peace in the experience
of what is to be appreciated.

3. moderation
Some of this, some of that
now and then, on a regular
basis with concentration.
Quality vs. Quantity should apply,
within one's means of course, to actually
enjoy and benefit from that
in which one desires with satisfaction.

4. maximization
Go all in it to win it.
Snatch and grab, hoard and
overreach. No! Put all into
success, enjoyment, reward
that can be mustered without offense? Yes!

5. extreme
Extremely out of whack out of balance, out of focus, out of reality, tainted perception or challenged by measures, and persevering.

NOBODY EVER LIKES A MOCKINGBIRD

Adam Ferreira

Real street shit,
Don't say a word.
On what you seen
Or what you heard.
Get your brains
Blown out on the curb,
'Cause nobody ever likes
A mockingbird.

Originally published in f(r)iction literary magazine, volume no.11 (Summer 2018)

ADDICTION

Mathematics Millionaire X

In my mother's womb was the greatest love

The nine letters in addiction mean I was hooked on drugs

Hustlers chase Gucci that brings groupie love

Prison is filled with violence, hate, gangs, and thugs

At the end of the day, everyone wants God's supreme love

Five times a day, Muslims pray on rugs

Forty dollars buys an addict a fix

Geto Boys said it best, our minds play tricks and become our worst enemy

A needle, cooker, and a crack pipe became best friends to me

Family love and support has always been there

The disease of addiction tells us no one cares

An addict's biggest problem is addressing their fears

Doing a drug to hide the heart's lack of love and care

If Hernandez worked the 12 Steps, I think he'd still be here

No matter the 1st, 2nd, or 3rd tier, the loss of hope and loneliness glooms in the air

There is a solution called the spiritual path

Giving 2 others 1st and putting our ego last

For a dollar a day, cutting prison grass, thinking about the past and our future paths

Prison is where you end up if you want to be a clown in class

Tired of the cold cereal during the Muslim fast

Takes reading and self-care to make this time in prison our last

Acts of kindness have more value than jewelry and cash

Life is fast like a car in the life of addiction

Mothers get the call their son or daughter has passed

Kids put flowers at the gravesite in the grass

This is not a game. Ask the families that have an addict's ashes in a glass

DON'T JUST SURVIVE

L. Marcel Harrison

Survival of the fittest, fastest, and most frustrated.
Survival of the most determined, focused, and greatest.
Survival of the most hated.
Survival of the most loved and appreciated.

Survival of the righteous,
the self, or not,
and survival of the charitable, humble, and modest too.
Survival of the degradation, insult, and victimization.

Survival of love, lust, and mistrust.
Survival of machination, glorification, and fabrication.
Survival of gossip and naysayers, religion,
politics, conspiracies, aliens, Darwinians,
and COINTELPRO.

Survival of schoolbooks that don't tell the truth
about Racism, feminism, stupidism, and eugenics too.
Matricide, patricide, questioning the lies.
Devised to mold the masses into a glob of congestion.
Don't just survive.

THE PROPHET OF POISON, II*

*Partially found poetry from Time Life Magazine,
March 20th, 2018*

Joel Thompson

But, by the most synthetic of catastrophes:
A poison created by man and a madness
that was strictly human. Heroin.

It was placed on urban streets
to simultaneously take people
to the darkest places of their lives.

Day after day, investigations would emerge
out of homes with this deadly chemical.

The perpetrators wore surgical masks
during this ordeal.

I saw several dozen people on the platform
who had either collapsed
or were on their knees unable to stand.

One man was thrashing around on the floor
like a fish out of water.

Three young women clung together
like small birds in a nest, trembling and crying,
yet made no sound.

The chemical had silenced their voices.

*The original Prophet of Poison, Shoko Asahara, founder of the doomsday cult, Aum Shinrikyo, was convicted for the 1995 sarin gas attack on the Tokoyo subway, as well as other crimes, and sentenced to death in 2004.

Originally published in f(r)iction literary magazine, volume no.11 (Summer 2018)

DISGUSTING

Brian Bellamy

My skin begun anew,
sloughing every seven years.
Burn, then peel.
My self evolves, melding,
dying, disquiet, life's desire.
Fall, failing,
my psyche is yearning.
Striving, strategic maneuvers,
plots, planning.
My soul's ending places.
Me, unable to cope, complete.

CONFESSIONS OF A COUCH POTATO

Malik Hall

My mind is stretched out
bouncing up and down.

I'm at risk, body never in motion
mind trapped in the backyard.

I'm at risk, notoriously known
to never stick to the basics.

Lifestyle choices have led
to a destiny known to me from past DNA.

What is my cure?
What was their cure?

A powerful drug,
A miracle drug.

Wow it worked.

My mood has improved.

SAW IT IN A DREAM

Mark Taylor

This is for real, saw it in a dream. Not sure
what it all means. Imagine possibilities, all
the lessons learned, many people helped in return.
Willing to work hard to live out the vision seen.

Images of battleships armed ready to engage.
Out of balance scales with uneven weights.
Armed citizens marching toward city
to take down iron gates.
Calluses on their hands, tired burning feet,
night's losing sleep, whatever it means,

they have a charge to keep. No more taking orders
from the powers that be. They're not willing to settle
for status quo. Though they look on in fear not knowing
what to do. The people are determined to stand
against every bleeping foe.

Running down Constitution Way, hoping

to find freedom that ends the struggle today.

Hoping to reach the passage where contentions

will be addressed, between the government

and the people,

people who want to keep them in check.

THE STILL

Barbara Lewis

It was 1925, the end of April, in a Georgia town that was a winter retreat for big name, big money families that summered in the grand cottages of Newport. Like birds, they flew south when the cold winds began to blow, and a more conducive climate was sought. It was mild and warm there, where Money Road met Leisure Street. The Rockefeller, Whitney, and Vanderbilt offspring spent their time playing cards, polo and golf, riding thoroughbreds, sipping bourbon, scotch, and rye, as they gossiped, danced, and dined away the hours.

Out on the tilled land, where corn ears waved tall in the wind, where mules furrowed the earth, Lon Samuelson prospered. He and his wife, Hilary, birthed eight children, and also took in nieces, nephews and cousins in need, making sure they all went to school every day with full bellies so they could learn and build a strong, new tomorrow. Lon, born in 1869, just after the Civil War, was good with numbers; he knew how to buy low and sell high. Year after year, favor smiled on the Samuelsons; and they tasted the kind of prosperity that, in their neighborhood, meant they felt no envy toward the Gilded families on the town's other side.

The shiny new Ford that Lon drove up and down the red clay roads, stirred up envy. So did the hundred-plus acres of farmland he owned. Must be those two sons of his, Dozier and Lester, the ones who went away to fight in that big war; they are the ones that turned the money tide for him. Lon was proud of his oldest boys, who had moved away, making themselves into new men with new views, living in a new city, up there in Harlem, where they found jobs, one as a hospital orderly and the other as a conductor on those underground trains that raced from station to station. Lon and Hilary visited New York once but couldn't wait to get back to what they knew. Cracked concrete under foot was fine for their sons, but they needed a closer relationship with the ground on which they walked.

    People, black and white, gossiped that the family kept a still. Old man Samuelson and his family made moonshine, they said. Every month or so one son or the other would drive down for the weekend and go back with their trunks full. That was how, people said, there was no end of new tools and livestock on their farm, helping Lon and Hilary get more acres, practically every year. Sooner or later, someone or something would trip them up and end it all. The Samuelson children dressed better than their friends at school. And the family had a new Ford; their bills were paid and they weren't on the short end of the stick at end-of-year time.

    To find out if the rumor that the Samuelsons had an illegal racket going was true, a sheriff and a deputy, all wearing plainclothes, arrived at the Samuelson spread one Saturday morning in April. They stationed themselves in the yard and began to shoot.

    Hilary Samuelson was cleaning up the kitchen after breakfast when a bullet whizzed through an open window, just inches away from her shoulder. Outside, her daughter, Mertis, was screaming. Rushing out to the back porch, Hilary peered around the corner of the house and saw Sheriff Howard and his deputy pistol whipping and kicking Mertis. Without a moment's thought, Hilary grabbed the rifle that Sam kept just inside the door. Howard and Deputy Richards saw the rifle in her hand and responded with a rain of bullets. *Hide*, Hilary said, as she fell, spending her last breath to warn her daughter. Mertis did what her mother said; she crawled under the house, hiding deep behind the brick pillars holding the structure high off the ground. In the darkness and dampness, Mertis lay bruised and wounded, cradling her stomach, comforting the new, growing life beating inside her, and doubling over, protecting the life within.

Returning from the grist mill, Lon Samuelson heard the shooting and knew what it meant. He had two choices; he could go home and see about his family or turn around the way he had come and drive the back roads until he found a neighbor or a relative who would take him in for a few days until he could get word to his sons in New York, almost a thousand miles away. He was on his own now.

Lon knew that a posse would be out soon looking for him. He would have to ditch his car and hide in the woods, eating berries and drinking from streams. They would set the dogs after him too. He had almost no chance of getting away. And he didn't.

The next day he was arrested. Then, he learned that his wife was gone and he was being charged with bootlegging. Even though no still was found on his property, his sentence was two years on the chain gang. Mertis, who had not lost her baby, Lon Jr., and Dennis, his nephew, were all charged with murdering the Sheriff. They insisted on their innocence but were not believed. Fred Jennings, a sympathetic lawyer and editor from Savannah, Georgia, took their case, clearing Dennis first. The bullets that killed Sheriff Howard were not buckshot, the only ammunition in the hunting rifles to which Dennis and Lon Jr. had access.

The night after Dennis was cleared of all charges, and it looked as if Mertis and Lon Jr. would also be exonerated in the sheriff's death, the local jail where they were being held was broken into, before dawn, and Mertis, Lon Jr., and Dennis were dragged, kicking and screaming, from their cells. Mertis Samuelson was still wearing her nightgown when she was delivered over to a procession of waiting cars. In the dark, the three Samuelsons were driven out of town, lynched and burned, in a clearing.

UNTITLED

Christine Arrington

The world goes on no matter what we say or do:
        Don't be afraid to let go

Let people know how strong you feel about something:
        They can agree or not, but you can still feel it

No matter how things may look, walk with your head up and go on
        No matter how you feel, you will not feel lonely

Don't be ashamed of your body and the way it looks
        Love it anyway

IV. WATER

AN OPEN LETTER TO ME, MYSELF, AND I

Tyson

Today, I'm learning how to sit with myself. It's been a very long time since I sat with myself. The only time I ever get to spend time with myself is when I go to jail and yet, when I find myself alone in a jail cell, I do everything I can to ignore myself. I always look for that negative attention just to make sure I keep running from the person that I'm really scared of.

I have to admit, life is pretty crazy and scary when a person doesn't know himself. I hate to say it, but the truth is that everyone that's been in my life, including the people still in my life, know me more than I know myself. A wise man once told me, "To know yourself, you have to start by loving yourself. To understand yourself, you have to believe in yourself." But everything starts with one thing and one thing only, respect.

When we have the willpower to respect ourselves, everything in us and around us will fall in place. Every day, people around the world struggle and suffer from many painful issues, and the only thing we know how to do best is either get high on some type of drug to numb our pain and escape reality, or we blame others for our mistakes and our pain, because we are so afraid to face our own selves.

The truth is that most human beings don't realize that our true enemy is ourselves, and our biggest fear is always accepting what we really are and who we really are. That is why it becomes easier to blame others for our wrongdoings and not ourselves. I've come to realize that one of the only ways for men and women to know themselves better is to grab a pen and paper and start writing about anything and many things.

HOPE FADE, TIME SLAYED

Ayanna Holder

Thou mighty howl of ancestral accent
orbs of wisdom tainted with the paint of the sea
looking into your soul seeing what light resides.
If you're awake or asleep
at last it goes as the present souls pay it no mind
letting yet another sliver of salvation slip by.
Thou shall never know of my treasures thy carried
nor of the crimson torch I bared in my soul
to guide you.

THE VISIT

Bassam Attia

Lost in the world
to the earth I am an orphan.
So much pain and anger,
I'm feeding my master's organ.
Feeling my temple, but then again
I'm soulless like a mannequin.
My ride has arrived. It's time to feel the pain.
Fuck!!! I'm in the place again.
The therapist claiming I'm insane,
but in my universe I'm sane.
In the end it all feels the same.
No pain, no gain, no gain, no game.
I just want someone to hear me!!!
Fuck the attention, I don't need fame.
Accepting death just as much as life,
abandonment became my wife.
Lonely in the world
feeling like I've already reached the afterlife,
with no one but my conscience to give
me advice.
Both wrists bleeding with the same blood,
I am my own potion's sacrifice,
still I continue to roll the dice.
Itching my head,
with memories and histories as if they
were lice.
The shadow in my room asking what's
the price?!!
As I look at him I'm drowning in tears,
filled with fears,
he looks into my soul's windows and smiles,
then as a dark cloud he slowly disappears,
but I still feel his presence for many years.

CHANCE ENCOUNTER[1]

Evan Jymaal Cutts

— *Dudley Square, Roxbury. April 7th, 2016*

I'm waiting in Dudley Square / it's late / and a man in his fifties going by / Eliot, walks up to me / tells me about a woman / this *crazy* woman / and their chance encounter on a stoop in Dorchester // She's a dancer / *tireless* and *tender*—but hard too // (imagine, she's gotta move like a fist) // clutching a sweetness / so tight this man pains himself to ignore her calls at twelve in the morning but doesn't // and finds himself here in Dudley / treading on two a.m. askin bout the 44 (needs to get to Brockton by eight) / except it don't run this late / (I don't tell him / say: *I'm a poet // just left a show*) then, he recites a poem / his own and another / but I can't understand his diction // admits he barely understands himself—no / it's gotta be the poems—the way they drag each line break out of him
                                      sometimes—
or all at once scares him shitless // I say: *writing poetry is like standing in front of a mirror—* / how our reflections might turn and shake us— / *'who wants, after all, to be seen too clearly?* // I tell him, poetry (for me) is an effort in translation / and I read to him about jokes that aren't jokes // about the blackbirds—their names dying in my throat / how our Sorrow Songs all became smoke // Dudley unveils crossroads of generations—and we, two Black men, pass time until well past when my bus was supposed to arrive // when I see it in the distance / preceded by the clamor and flash of police sirens / I confess my

---

[1] With a line from "Dhaka Nocturne" by Tarfia Faizullah

sadness / at the sound / too much of Roxbury is this song—of those led to their drowning // As it turns into the station, I ask for his number—*as fellow poets* // and He looks me in the eyes / smiles—light / says // *Sure, but I don't know / if I'll ever pick up.*

Originally published in The Offing Magazine, November 1, 2018, as "Encounters: Dudley Square"

EVANS IS A POET: A LITERARY ANALYSIS OF "CHANCE ENCOUNTER"

Anthony Calhoun

Evans is a poet waiting on the last bus in Dudley Station. As he's waiting for the bus, thinking about his show, and correlating his experience with his standing at a bus stop in Boston, late at night, he begins to think. Evans, possibly in recovery himself, believes the man is possibly approaching him to game him for money or a ride to his destination. The man tells Evans about a dancer to distract Evans or feel him out from what he was really trying to do. But the man discovers the way the conversation was going and probably thought that Evans was probably hip to him and that Evans gave him his number to try to get him to a meeting.

WHISTLER'S NOCTURNE

Debbie Wiess

Nocturne: In Blue and Gold
Oh, the mysteries and wonder you do hold!
Myriad gradations of midnight and indigo blue
infused with the faintest hints of golden hue.
Influenced perhaps by Turner and Hiroshige,
but with your own originality springing
from Whistler's inimitable creativity.

Old wooden bridge of Battersea, whose
darkened lattice legs stretch across at Chelsea
between the Thames' uneven shores
in you is most eerily depicted.
Surrounded by constant comings and goings,
the buzz of beehive-like maritime activity.
Now at the end of another busy day
a return of quiet and tranquility.
Lights of the city and in the heavens
pierce through the thickened night air.
A single soul tends to his day's final efforts
twilight glimmering upon the crests
of the river's lapping waves.

O'er the scene high up in the sky
an atmospheric phenomena, dense
and hazy, hangs heavily upon invisible rods,
like a sheer steel grey scrim upon a stage.
The perceptible mist of dirt and particles,
result of early industry on land and sea,
that once choked lungs and blinded
eyes of London's inhabitants
though creating an ambiance both

enigmatic and most romantic.
Long gone may be this mechanized fog,
but so too the charm, hard to deny,
that it also produced, inspiring greatly
writers, poets and artists all.

Little understood when first painted
so much ridicule did you withstand
from critics, populace and most of all
Ruskin, fellow artist and arbiter of taste
so idolized and adored in his day.
It was he who led the charge of insults,
accusing poor Whistler in creating you,
of flinging upon the public's face a pot of paint.
Proud Whistler, not surprisingly, was
rankled, taking exception to the foul claims.
Leading to a suit against Ruskin for libel.
Won at last after lengthy testimony and
debate of Whistler's craft and style.
Garnering the artist but a single farthing
in the end for all his troubles.
Financial ruin was thought his fate
'til came to him a new commission.
Off to Venice he was sent posthaste
a series of water colors he to paint.
Leading him to new-found acclaim,
he no longer to hang his head in shame.

O, Nocturne: In Blue and Gold,
painting which once so affronted
and for many years remained unsold,
now with pride in the Tate Britain do reside.
You and other nocturnes equally mocked,
today are most revered and prized.
Sealing talented Whistler's fame and
place in the pantheon among the greats.

As is the beauty of a butterfly remarked
so too the genius of Whistler at last recognized
once released from the cocoon of misconceptions.

UNTITLED I

Daniel

She enters you slowly
and pleasurable.
She's pricey goodtime,
no bars hold, manipulative.
Shiny things, down to take
anything. Nickname is *Widowmaker*.
She's undefeated. Hold the belt
tight against her like the hold
she puts on you once you
get her fully released into
you, unforgiveable, drama filled,
leaves you broken and poor
once she drains your soul,
leaves your family out in the
cold. You'll cross her path.
She'll come with a reaper's
grasp.

YET ANOTHER EXQUISITE CORPSE

Wyman, Group 2, Tuesday, 10:30 a.m.

The heroin enters the man's bloodstream.
A second ago he was sick.
Now he can walk on water.
Now he can start the day.

The voice always becomes strangely
calm. Breathing slows to a crawl.

I'm in another world,
about to dance at Studio 54,
play football in the Super Bowl,
go to the White House,
drink tea, talk to the President. Wow,
this heroin is gorgeous.

I hope it lasts because I'm almost out.
I want to stay in this paradise,
away from my reality.

Maybe I can go to Florida,
go to Disneyworld,
and play a few rounds
with Donald at his country club.

IN THE OCEAN

City World

In the ocean is where I want my ashes spread,
like my ancestors who jumped from the ship
because they knew that death was better than life
in bondage.

AS DEEP AS EARTH BELOW THE OCEAN

Bruce DiGaetano, II

When thoughts cross a brain,
it's as if they're drops of rain.
Slowly, they fill oceans, but deeper,
until they become steady, yet weaker.
These thoughts ruminate
until they germinate
like seeds of seagrass on the ocean floor.
Some can be crass and some can bore
deeper and deeper into a person's core.
Nurtured by water, they're both sustained
by words on paper and drops of rain.
All distinguished by thoughts crossing a brain.

SPAWN SEASON

Adam Ferreira

It's spawn season and momma fish laid 100,000 eggs. Daddy fish fertilized them just before an eagle swooped down and snatched him out of the water, and then half of the eggs got eaten by a sunfish. A month later, there's 50,000, and we hatch into little fishes and part ways. 10,000 are eaten by turtles, 20,000 by other fish, 15,000 die from lack of food, and 4,000 of us were big enough to not be bullied too easy. But, one day, I saw this real shiny fish ahead of me and, suddenly, I got pulled out the water and in the air and everything went dark.

HAT'KEYAH: GRUMPY JEW POEM #89

Sara Willig

October 29, 2018
20 Heshvan 5779

Sometimes, I fear I lead a shallow life.
A timid glance directed t'wards a tide pool.
The dun mare, Anxiety, thunders always past me.
It's hard to be a squeaky wheel
when every ounce of energy is expended
avoiding the sound.
Attention narrows to a sharpened point.
Depression hems my world.
Problematic body, needle sharp mind.
My thoughts embroider snippets of better worlds.
Tikun Olam my T'keyah.

POETIC MEDICINE

Joel Reyes, Jr.

Bring me the real,
you holders, you beacons.
Process is the point.
I know your kind,
a wolf calling a wolf a wolf.
As the world gets weirder
and weirder,
imagination is under pressure.
We are diving through windows,
reconnecting after silence
at new paths to the waterfalls.
With ideas for an inspired new year,
the place for your poem is here!
Publish your passion.
You are not alone.
Write to be read.

V. OUR CONTRIBUTORS

artwork by Bruce DiGaetano, II

Zachary Alonzo is a recovering heroin addict and convicted felon, but don't judge a book by its cover. After being released from state prison, while in a six-month reentry program, he picked up writing, which has helped him expand his mind and been a good outlet to aid in his recovery. Zach has also served as a Primary Trainer for New England Assisted Dog Services for people with PTSD, special needs, and disabilities; a member of Prison Voices, speaking to high school students; and a Lead Facilitator with the Correctional Recovery Academy addressing drug abuse and violence. Look for him in the documentary *In Their Shoes: Unheard Stories of Reentry and Recovery*, due for release in early 2019.

Christine Arrington is a person who lives in Boston and does very well. She is a member of art classes and enjoys making beautiful things, but she is not a member of a group. She likes to collect books and pens. She enjoys seeing horror movies and going to baseball games with people. She believes all people are created equal and should not be judged by other people who are so negative about everything they talk about. She likes to surround herself with positive people.

Bassam Attia is an artist and poet raised in Portugal and the United States. He was brought up Christian, but is now a practicing Muslim. He speaks four languages (English, Spanish, Portuguese, and Cape Verdean Creole), has traveled to seven countries, and is obsessed with history and mythology, all of which he weaves through his artwork. He's interested in using faith and self-expression to empower youth, helping them become better people and leaders in their communities through their art.

Brian Bellamy is a lifelong resident of the Bay State. A "Masshole" whose only fealty is to the Red Sox Nation, he's also a man who despises those who refer to themselves in the third person. His political views are somewhere between Anarchist and Social Democrat. He is trying to be a better father, brother, and friend. His hobbies include fishing, reading, and talking to people he likes. He also attempts to write.

Cheryl Blanchard is a recovering addict. She is from Cambridge and now resides in Jamaica Plain. She has lived a very colorful life—ups and downs, and ins and outs of this thing called "life." However, now she lives a wonderful sober life, sharing and giving of herself. She loves collecting angels and baking. God has blessed her with many gifts. In this thing called life, wisdom works wonders.

Kay Bluelondon writes and sings to challenge and encourage herself and others to look more deeply at their own journey and connection with the world. She is an artist who explores power to illuminate the darkest places. She believes that we all fall sometimes and some fall even deeper, but if she could get up you can too. Kay believes that poems can change lives and the way we think and behave regarding the most critical matters of our time.

Karen Brogan enjoys the Writers Without Margins group. She enjoys the different activities, including art. She likes watching TV, especially *In the Heat of the Night*. However, she prefers being around people rather than staying in her room watching TV or doing crosswords. She likes to go out when the weather is permissible and that is why her favorite season is summer.

Andrew Burlile holds an MA in Irish Studies from Boston College, focusing on gendered language in transnational contexts as represented in contemporary Irish literature. He began writing in his early teens, and after completing his first novel at 16, which far from being, as he claimed at the time, "the best novel this side of the Atlantic," he has all but abandoned the project in pursuit of other projects which he may also abandon depending on how the day's going. He's currently working on his "real first novel," which explores the intersections of race, language, and historical privilege in a southern Virginia community. His favorite writers currently are Toni Morrison, Maggie Nelson, and William Faulkner. And, George Saunders and Annie Dillard, Frank Bidart, bell hooks, Gloria Anzaldúa, Alice Munro, Tommy Orange, and Alice Walker. He hopes one day to write like them. Though he would never articulate it outright, he's motivated by prestige and awards and people telling him his work is good even though he doesn't believe them. He believes he'll eventually write something great. Until then, he plans to continue writing every day, reaffirming to himself the power and conviction of literature.

Anthony Calhoun is a person trying to bridge his many experiences of the City of Boston into a meaningful business plan to start a contemporary business that the city can truly benefit from.

Michael K. Capriola, Jr.'s hobbies include reading, writing and drawing.

City World is a self-made hustler who is wiser than he used to be because of the trials and tribulations he has survived. He believes in the future. He recognizes the comfort of isolation but warns that we never get too lost in it, wanting rather to emphasize the importance of being his brother's keeper. Always, being his brother's keeper.

Stephen Crivellaro was born and raised in Beaufort, South Carolina. He has an affinity for the outdoors, a genuine appreciation for fine literature, and a firm belief that dreams are tangible, no matter how big or small, through patience, persistence, and perseverance. He has two beautiful children, a boy and a girl, currently two and seven years old, respectively. He resides in Eastern Massachusetts, where he intends to continue furthering his education.

Evan Jymaal Cutts is a 24-year-old Boston native, poet, journalist, and writing workshop facilitator. Evan was a member of the Emerson College 2017 CUPSI Team and 2017 National Poetry Slam "Last Chance Slam" Team. He puts his faith in Black joy, his mother and father, and the power of imagination. His poetry navigates expressions of Blackness, Boston, mythology, and magic. His poetry is published in *Broken Head Press*, *Apogee Journal*, *Voicemail Poems*, *Maps for Teeth*, and *The Merrimack Review*. Evan will be pursuing his MFA in Creative Writing at Rutgers University - Newark as a Chancellor's MFA Mentors Program Fellow. Follow him on Facebook @cuttsartistry & on Instagram @fg_cutts.

Daniel was a kind and supportive member of our community who always brought his best to the writing workshop. In August, he passed away from a fatal drug overdose at age 39. He is not forgotten.

Bruce DiGaetano, II is from Chelsea. He's had a long journey to get to this point in life, and all he can say is keep your eye on the prize and never give up. Good luck to all in your battles though they are not easy. If you can make it through the night, there's a brighter day.

Adam Ferreira is from New Bedford, and is a person who struggled with making the right choices in life before learning to express himself in positive ways. He made some bad choices, which led to the hard struggle. Nothing changes, though, if nothing changes, and he's working on changing a lot.

Beatrice Greene, born in the South Bronx to African American parents, is a poet, composer, pianist, trumpeter, and dramatist. She delights in convening community open mics with themes such as *Images Outside the Box: Defining Beauty for Ourselves, Place and Transitions.* Her poems include social justice, humor, theology, science and nature themes. Her published poetry may be found in *The Bones We Carry*, Streetfeet Press, 2009; *Lunar Calendar* 2016, 2019 and *Extra Mojo!* Hidden Charm Press, 2013; *Writers Without Margins, Vol. III, Lost and Found Edition,* 2018. Beatrice performs a one woman show presenting the poetry and life of Frances E. Watkins Harper, nineteenth-century black woman abolitionist, lecturer and author. In 2016, she composed and performed a piano composition, called *The Other,* at Roxbury Community College. Beatrice enjoys astrophysics, water color painting, practicing Spanish, cooking for friends and hiking in her spare moments. She belongs to the Time Project, an experimental women artists group.

Malik Hall is a recovering addict. He is a very passionate, honest person and, for the first time, his mind is open for suggestions. He is finally willing to love himself enough to show himself he can live like a positive, normal human being.

Lisa Harding is a member of a writing group in Jamaica Plain. In college she took a creative writing course. She likes poetry, art and music. She has traveled to England, Arizona, Florida, Washington, and New Jersey. She enjoys making collages and has sold some of them.

L. Marcel Harrison has been to hell, and yet he does have some notion of what it feels like to experience heaven here on earth. He finds himself in balance between the two realms today. He hopes to share wisdom through the medium of literature as the result of his journey.

Ayanna Holder is a city girl and a child of nature. Her musical taste ranges from around the world, including opera and classical. Her favorite book is *Krsna: The Supreme Personality of Godhead*, through which she has learned how the material world can trap us, how we can break free, and the roles of destiny, reincarnation and choice, and she hasn't even finished all 900 pages. Ayanna aspires to someday live in a mini-manor in the woods among her brothers and sisters amidst her larger family of living things, the animals and the trees.

Barbara Lewis heads the William Monroe Trotter Institute for the Study of African Diaspora History and Culture at the University of Massachusetts-Boston, where she is an Associate Professor of English, with publications on lynching, the nineteenth-century minstrel stage, the Black Arts Era of the Sixties, and the urban drama of August Wilson. A translator and co-translator of work written in French pertaining to Francophone drama, literature, and theory, Dr. Lewis is focused, currently, on creative memoir, featuring her southern maternal and northern paternal families. Jeremiah Bradley, her northern great-great-grandfather, fought in the legendary 54th Massachusetts, championed by Frederick Douglass, lionized in the Hollywood film *Glory*, and memorialized in bronze by the Irish sculptor, Augustus Saint Gaudens, across from the Massachusetts State House.

Mathematics Millionaire X is a man that grew up in Cambridge, Boston, detox holdings, halfway houses, and the state prison system. Coming from a great family and a nurturing upbringing, he got caught up in the game of the streets. His mother is his everything, and trying to recover, on a daily basis with humility, is his goal in life.

T. O'Malley was born in the middle of a turbulent decade, coming to light in an Irish Catholic family, dirt poor and scraping by, somehow, thanks to his barely literate immigrant father whose work ethic was legendary, along with his alcohol and spousal abuse. The epitome of lost middle child syndrome, T. disappeared in the success of his brothers' accomplishments, stature, and popularity, committing himself instead to petty crimes ranging from hooking school to petty larceny. School held little interest, aside from being a destination where the girls congregated, nor did any of its subjects, other than English Literature where he discovered a natural talent for reading and writing, a talent which his drinking brought out nightly.

Laura Price has lived all her life in Boston. Born in Lowell on September 9, 1966, she has a high school diploma, but never went to college. She has an excellent ability to learn new things. She likes crocheting, doing puzzles, playing different types of games, and taking challenges that might be hard but she does the best she can to succeed at. She has a good rapport with people, gets along with everyone, and tries to do everything she is asked to do. She has had a number of pets throughout the years. She has had apartments but has lost them all. She knows she will get one eventually in the future. She just takes one day at a time and braces for whatever comes. She's also a mother.

Kevin Reddick grew up in Boston as the son of Yolanda and the brother of seven siblings. An aspiring writer and poet, he also has a CDL license, likes basketball, and enjoys listening to music.

Joel Reyes, Jr. passed briefly through a Writers Without Margins workshop, offered thoughtful contributions to the discussion, and left behind a beautiful poem for our collection. (Thanks, Joel.)

Martin Rodriguez grew up on the Jersey Shore. After graduating from Harvard, he fell in love with Boston, where his poetry was exhibited at City Hall. He is most recently published in the *Paterson Literary Review*, and has read his poems on television, the Massachusetts Poetry Festival, Copley Square library, and other venues.

William Sharp was born in Taunton, February 20, 1975. He is 205 pounds of twisted steel and sex appeal. 34 inches in the waist, and kind of cute in the face, often imitated, and rarely duplicated. He's been through way too many wars to explain, and writing keeps him sane.

M.R. Shipp has not much education but is a great lover of knowledge. Born a Midwesterner, he has been an Easterner for a long time. He believes no building is as dazzling as our Boston Public Library and he has surrendered for years to its intricate and sustainable charm! He would like the ancestors to allow his death to happen while reading a good book, physical or digital, and listening to music.

Mark Taylor grew up in Boston in a large family as the sixth child of thirteen where it was quite difficult to get the attention that he desired. So, he had to figure out where in the world did he fit. He spent a lot of time by himself, observing, trying to give his input, but often felt left out, unheard. Writing became like a good friend because he could look back later, and the words would speak to him and he would listen. He graduated from high school, joined the Marine Corps, was honorably discharged, got married, had four children, got divorced, and experienced homelessness. Life goes on. But, he still wonders, where in the world do I fit?

Joel Thompson was born in Brooklyn, NY, but raised in New Bedford. Seven county and two state bids later, he is at peace with himself. After battling drug addiction and abuse for years, he is still haunted by the past. To confront it, he focuses on his writing, which he enjoys. He wants to tell anyone who has been to the belly of the beast — there is hope and peace out there, but you have to work for it and never give up.

Tyson, a writer, a father, and a Yankees fan, is originally from Puerto Rico. He believes in building connections by working between and within communities, with youth, and channeling positivity.

Debbie Wiess is a Boston-based writer, who writes in French, as well as English. She has created a wide array of pieces for stage and screen, and poetry, in both languages. Her work has been presented around the U.S. and abroad in traditional theatres and alternative spaces. Her poetry has been published on several continents. One poem along with two of her short plays were included in a textbook on International Creative Writing published in the Philippines. She was a guest artist at the 2010 Kennedy Center Playwrights' Intensive and was a participant in the Great Plains Theatre Conference in 2007 with her 10-minute play ONE MORE TO GO. In addition to writing, she directs and produces projects and events. This will be the first time her work has appeared in the *Writers Without Margins* Journal.

Sara Willig is anxious, Autistic, and almost 50; it's probably an over-sized amygdala. She lives nowhere near a Starbucks in one of the less commercialized corners of Cambridge in a Section 8. When hiding from the world, Sara watches TV, doesn't do housework, and recently acquired a specialized MPA. She was appalled to discover herself an accidental Business Major, as she was only in it for the skills to enable her to subvert and/or topple the Paradigm.

William attended a workshop for a while before employment got in the way. He shared his work and his wisdom and then moved on. (Thank you, William)

Cles A. Wilson, a native of New England, lives in Massachusetts in the heart of the city, where the weather is always a hot topic. As a writer, she enjoys writing short stories, poems, and free speech. Cles is also an inspired Spoken Word artist, as well as growing in her leadership role as an encourager. To quote, the quote: "I never know when a prose or a story is going to grab me, so I keep plenty of napkins on hand."

VI. OUR PARTNERS

Bridge Over Troubled Waters (Boston) is Boston's premier organization dedicated to transforming the lives of runaway, homeless, and high-risk youth through safe, supportive, and encouraging relationships and effective and innovative services that guide them toward self-sufficiency. Programs include: street outreach and mobile medical vans, runaway hotlines, counselors, and emergency overnight accommodations for teens, support services, survival aid, day programs, in-house medical and dental clinics, education and career development, emergency residence, transitional living programs and single parent housing for pregnant and parenting homeless young women and their children. Since the 1970s, Bridge remains a national model and program incubator for youth development services which are effective in helping the most troubled and vulnerable homeless youth to turn their lives around.

The Center for Change (Dorchester) was an adult day health program licensed by the Department of Public Health and operated by Kit Clark Senior Services, a division of Bay Cove Human Services. This program was geared specifically for adults who were experiencing homelessness and for those who had been recently housed. Participants received nursing support to maintain their health and well-being, participate in social and recreational activities, and receive nutritional meals as well as ongoing social services. Participants also received case management support to secure health insurance, housing, benefits, and other individual objectives. The Center strived to improve the quality of life of a population who faced lifelong challenges of aging, mental illness, addiction and homelessness. Many of the participants in the Center for Change, with the supports from our staff and Boston Health Care for the Homeless, had successes with finding housing, maintaining sobriety and securing employment. The Center was defunded in 2018.

The Boston Public Library (Greater Boston), established in 1848 by an act of the Great and General Court of Massachusetts, is the first large, free, municipal library in the United States. In the latter half of the nineteenth century, the BPL began developing its branch system to include its 25 diverse, neighborhood libraries, which exist today throughout Greater Boston, with one central location in Copley Square. The award-winning renovations at the central branch include a state of-the-art lecture hall, business library and innovation center, a new Children's Library and Teen Central, a WGBH satellite news bureau and studio, a café, a high-tech community learning center, and more. To date, Writers Without Margins has run workshops partnering with Copley Square, East Boston, Dudley Square, Codman Square and Grove Hall.

St. Francis House (Boston), located in the heart of downtown Boston, serves an average of 500 poor and homeless men and women a day, 365 days a year. Its basic, rehabilitative, and housing services overlap and build on one another to provide guests with continuous and comprehensive care. Their mission is: St. Francis House rebuilds lives by providing refuge and pathways to stability for adults experiencing homelessness and poverty. St. Francis House is a welcoming and inclusive community. Every day of the year, we enable individuals to meet their basic needs for food, clothing and shelter. We transform lives using a holistic approach to understanding and addressing behavioral health, housing and employment needs. We commit ourselves to helping those we serve achieve renewed lives of dignity and self-determination.

The Pine Street Inn (Jamaica Plain) provides a comprehensive range of services, including permanent supportive housing, job training and placement, emergency shelter and street outreach to nearly 2,000 homeless men and women each day. 115 unsheltered homeless men and women are served daily by workers on foot and by van. Pine Street is the only organization that provides nighttime outreach in Boston. Founded in 1969, Pine Street is the largest resource for homeless men and women in New England. Clinical psychiatric staff and specialized programs provide support to nearly 50% of Pine Street's guests and 30% of tenants. Post-detox and other recovery programs, including the Stabilization Program, are also offered to those in need.

The Wyman Recovery Home (Mattapan) is operated by the Boston Public Health Commission's Recovery Services Bureau (BRS). It is a 30 bed, evidence-based, 4- to 6-month residential substance use treatment program for men. The goal of the Wyman Recovery Home is to offer a safe and therapeutic environment that supports residents in their recovery. The Wyman Recovery Home provides services twenty-four hours a day, seven days per week and focus on relapse prevention, behavior modification, interpersonal skill development, as well as re-socialization skills. Facilitated client discussion groups meet daily to explore life issues related to substance use. Services at Wyman include: substance use counseling, case management, assistance with recovery supports and aftercare planning and referrals.

VII. OUR MISSION

Writers Without Margins, Inc. is dedicated to the fusion of art and advocacy, taking literature beyond conventional spaces. Our mission is to expand access to the literary arts for unheard and under-resourced communities in Greater Boston — including those isolated by the challenges of addiction recovery, trauma, poverty, disability, and mental illness — through free collaborative writing workshops, public readings, and publication opportunities intended to empower communities, amplify the voices of individuals, and share their stories with the world.

To learn more, join us, order journals, or support our mission, visit us at: **writerswithoutmargins.org**

To my Spiritual Mother

Appreciate the love and all you've done for me. Thank you much

Sky'a

Made in the USA
Middletown, DE
06 March 2019